SdKfz 251 Ausf D

Walk Around

Hans-Heiri Stapfer

Ab 1942
Panzergrenadiertruppe

Squadron Signal
Publications

Covers and profiles by Don Greer
Illustrations by Matheu Spraggins

Introduction

The most important Wehrmacht (German Army) armored half-track in World War II (WWII) was the Sonderkraftfahrzeug 251 (special purpose vehicle 251 or SdKfz 251) Mittlerer Schützenpanzerwagen (medium armored personnel carrier). The Third Reich built no other armored vehicle in such substantial numbers. A total of 15,252 SdKfz 251s were produced in four modifications and 23 variants with the last main production modification being the SdKfz 251 Ausf D (Ausf is the abbreviation for Ausführung/model designation). Ausf D manufacturing started in early 1943, and lasted until March 1945, by which time 10,602 SdKfz 251 Ausf Ds were already built and represented nearly 70 percent of all the SdKfz 251 vehicle models produced during the war. These large production numbers were possible because the Ausf D's Panzergehäuse (armored superstructure) was simplified to speed up vehicle production. During 1944, the Ausf D model totaled 7,785 vehicles, approximately half the total SdKfz 251 production and nearly three quarters of the Ausf D wartime production.

The SdKfz 251 chassis was built by a number of automotive companies such as Auto Union, Adler Werke, Hannoversche Maschinenbau AG (Hanomag), and Škoda. Also, different factories in the Third Reich manufactured the Panzergehäuse. The chassis and armor body subsequently were mated in a final vehicle assembly plant, where four such assembly lines were established.

A crew of 12 manned the SdKfz 251 Ausf D armored personnel carrier. The driver and commander sat up front under an armored roof, and the rest of the crew rode in the open-top crew compartment at the rear of the half-track. A large double door, also at the rear of the vehicle, gave the troops access to this crew compartment.

The hull front had 14.5 mm armor protection. Both the superstructure's sides had 8 mm armor plates, and the vehicle's roof and floor had 5.5 mm armor plates. The armor protected crew members from small arms and artillery fragments.

The Ausf D had an overall length of 5.8 meters and a gross weight of 8.5 metric tons. A Maybach HL 42 TUKRRM 6-cylinder, water-cooled engine with 100 horsepower (hp) provided the half-track with a 52 km/h maximum road speed and a 20 km/h maximum off-road speed.

The SdKfz 251 saw action on every front, carried Panzergrenadier-Kompanien (armored infantry companies) into combat, and supported retreating Third Reich Panzer forces until the Germans surrendered in May 1945.

(Front Cover) This SdKfz 251/7 Ausf D engineer vehicle served the 12. SS-Panzer Division *Hitlerjugend* that fought against Allied forces in France. Two assault rails are mounted on supporting brackets on the superstructure.

(Back Cover) Elements of the Panzer Grenadier Division *Grossdeutschland* launch an assault in East Prussia during mid-January 1945. An SdKfz 251/9 provides cover for the troops by firing at enemy targets.

About the Walk Around®/On Deck Series®

The Walk Around®/On Deck® series is about the details of specific military equipment using color and black-and-white archival photographs and photographs of in-service, preserved, and restored equipment. *Walk Around* titles are devoted to aircraft and military vehicles, while *On Deck* titles are devoted to warships. They are picture books of 80 pages, focusing on operational equipment, not one-off or experimental subjects.

Copyright 2008 Squadron/Signal Publications
1115 Crowley Drive, Carrollton, TX 75006-1312 U.S.A.
Printed in the U.S.A.

ISBN 978-0-89747-575-4

Military/Combat Photographs and Snapshots

If you have any photos of aircraft, armor, soldiers, or ships of any nation, particularly wartime snapshots, please share them with us and help make Squadron/Signal's books all the more interesting and complete in the future. Any photograph sent to us will be copied and returned. Electronic images are preferred. The donor will be fully credited for any photos used. Please send them to:

Squadron/Signal Publications
1115 Crowley Drive
Carrollton, TX 75006-1312 U.S.A.
www.SquadronSignalPublications.com

Acknowledgements

Ruedi Bühler, Deutsches Panzermuseum Munster at Munster (Federal Republic of Germany), Nadine Fuchs of the Munster Tourist Office, Walter Grube, Kerstin Gutbrod, Esther and Thomas Hug, Schweizerisches Militärmuseum at Full (Switzerland), Willfried Rorig.

All photos of the SdKfz 251/7 Ausf D and SdKfz 251/9 Ausf D published in this book were taken during October 2007 by the author in the Deutsches Panzermuseum (German Armor Museum), Hans-Krüger-Strasse 33, D-29633 Munster, Germany.

(Title Page) These Schützenpanzerwagen (armored personnel carriers) are exhibited at the Deutsches Panzermuseum (German Armor Museum) at Munster in Northern Germany. On the left is an SdKfz 251/7 Ausf D Mittlerer Pionierpanzerwagen, an assault engineer vehicle. On the right is an SdKfz 251/9 Ausf D with a single Sturmkanone KwK 37 L/24 75 mm gun. The United States (U.S.) Army captured both vehicles during WWII, and they traveled to the U.S. for evaluation. Eventually, the vehicles were returned to Germany and restored by specialists of the Bundeswehr (Army of the Federal Republic of Germany) and the Deutsches Panzermuseum.

The SdKfz 251/9 Ausf D is an unusual example of the gun-equipped Schützenpanzerwagen. This particular vehicle has front fenders that were featured on the Ausf C variant. Very few early production SdKfz 251 Ausf Ds were equipped with the Ausf C front fenders. These fenders had a bent front, which was eliminated on most Ausf D models to speed up production. Another unusual characteristic for this model are the metal caps on the tracks, which were briefly used during summer 1944. Most Ausf D models had hard rubber pads attached on the tracks and were powered by a Maybach HL 42 TUKRRM six-cylinder, water-cooled engine with an output of 100 hp that provided the half-track with a power-to-weight ratio of 11.7 hp per ton. As an armored personnel carrier, the SdKfz 251 enabled the infantry to keep up with the Wehrmacht's fast armored elements. The Schützenpanzerwagen protected the infantry from enemy gun fire and strong points, and the infantry protected these vehicles from close-in attacks by enemy anti-tank formations. The cooperation between tanks and infantry enabled an attack at great speed and with limited casualties on both formations.

SdKfz 251 Ausf D Design Evolution

SdKfz 251/1 Ausf D (early)—First production vehicles were manufactured in early 1943 and had 12 crew members. They were equipped with a position light on the left and right front fender. The Ausf D had a straight rear plate and simple doors and was the first SdKfz 251 model equipped with three stowage bins on both sides of the lower superstructure.

SdKfz 251/1 Ausf D (standard)—This vehicle's main design difference removed the position lights from the front fenders to speed up production, and most vehicles lacked a reflector under the left rear fender. Early and standard production vehicles had a Notek blackout light on the left front fender. The rubber-rimmed wheels' coverings had a flat surface. In 1944, the fuel tank's dimensions were changed, and the original 130-watt Bosch generator was replaced by a 300-watt generator. Externally, these two features were not visible.

SdKfz 251/1 Ausf D (late)—The late production vehicle had the Notek blackout light replaced by a Bosch light mounted on the left front fender. The electrical wire changed positions and ran under the fender and into the chassis. The cover of the rubber-rimmed outer wheels and the idler had a depression imprinted into the cap. Late production SdKfz 251 Ausf Ds had the MG 34 7.92 mm machine gun replaced by an MG 42 machine gun of the same caliber, which resulted in an extension of the swing arm mounted on top of the rear superstructure. Most late production half-tracks had a reflector attached under the left rear fender. No reflector was ever attached under the right rear fender.

SdKfz 251/7 Ausf D Mittlerer Pionierpanzerwagen—This vehicle had an eight-person crew and was an assault engineer vehicle with support brackets on both sides of the superstructure. These brackets usually carried two Übergangsschienen 8 (8 metric ton bridge sections), which were used to bridge trenches or large shell holes. Some vehicles had the space between the brackets filled with wooden planking.

SdKfz 251/9 Ausf D—This version had a 7.5 cm KwK 37 L/24 gun that provided close support with heavy firepower for the Panzergrenadier (armored infantry) units. The front plate above the commander's seat was cut out for the gun, and a 52-round ammunition supply was carried for the gun. The crew consisted of three soldiers.

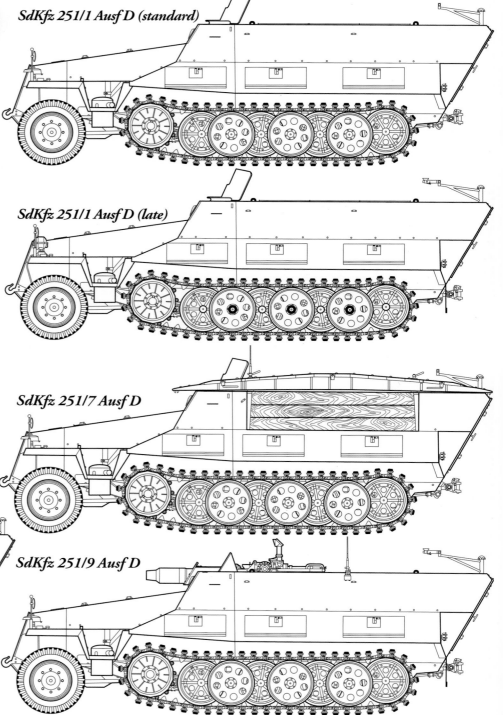

SdKfz 251/1 Ausf D (standard)

SdKfz 251/1 Ausf D (late)

SdKfz 251/7 Ausf D

SdKfz 251/9 Ausf D

SdKfz 251/1 Ausf D (early)

The front armor plate was 14.5 mm thick, and the circular aperture in the lower front of this armor plate was for the starting crank. A circular fairing covered this opening on most Ausf Ds. In fact during Wehrmacht operation, the circular covering was often deleted, and the last Ausf D production batches eliminated this cover at the assembly line.

The small, lower armor plates protected the steering arm and the lower part of the radiator, which was cooled by two fans.

Two distinctive features for the majority of SdKfz 251 Ausf Ds was the straight fender design and a rear view mirror that was mounted only on the left boom to make vehicle production faster. While early production Ausf Ds had a position light mounted on the left and right fenders between the Notek blackout light and the boom, the standard production vehicle did not have these lights.

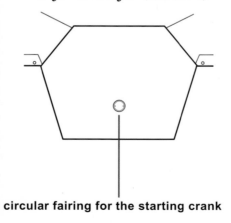

This view of the left towing hook shows the hook's pin and the three bolts that secure it to the vehicle's lower armor body. Both the left and right towing hooks were identically made and assembled.

Front Armor Development

SdKfz 251 Ausf D (standard)

circular fairing for the starting crank

SdKfz 251 Ausf D (late)

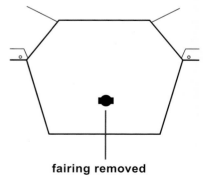

fairing removed

The towing hooks, located on the front section's left and right side, were each secured to the lower armor body by three bolts—an Ausf D feature never redesigned throughout the half-track's entire production cycle. Most of these hooks came with a pin. These hooks, which obstacles frequently bent or broke, proved necessary features in the Soviet Union where vehicles were frequently in need of being pulled free from the muddy roads.

The front axle of the SdKfz 251 Ausf D was forged from steel, was supported by a transverse elliptical spring (on top of the axle), was 65 mm high, and had two spring retainers secured by a pin. The Ausf D's axle design remained unchanged throughout the vehicle's production cycle.

This view shows the right front axle of a late production SdKfz 251/7 with taller screws securing the front axle to the lower surface.

This view features the left front axle of an early production SdKfz 251/9 with smaller screws fixing the front axle.

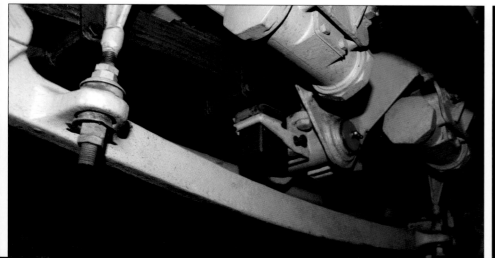

This view highlights the right-side front tire and its rim. The front wheels were 575 mm in diameter and had no brake system. The tires consisted of synthetic rubber called Buna, which used brown coal as its base. Beginning in 1937, the IG Farbenindustrie AG produced Buna in large quantities since the Third Reich did not have access to natural rubber from the Far East.

This right, front tire shot gives close-up access to the inner rim. The rims were made from pressed steel, and the right axis lacked a steering arm.

This view focuses on the right suspension unit, the straight, front fender—a common vehicle feature that made production faster—and the right-side front tire. The Ausf D had a 32 cm ground clearance and a 12.5 meter turning radius.

This assembly is the left, front axle's steering arm ball joint with its steering pin. Also note the laminated spring.

Some front tires had air valves. The 9.75-20 inch front tires were heavy duty and had an air pressure of 2.25 atmospheres. Solid, synthetic rubber tires also were used on the vehicle, but these tires did not have an air valve.

Only the left, front axle had a steering arm. Beveled gearing connected the steering wheel to the steering column, and the steering box, which regulated steering operations, was situated on the left side of the frame. The road track suspension units were on swing arms with transverse torsion bars.

The **SdKfz 251 Ausf D** could carry tools on the upper surface of both fenders although a number of vehicles did not carry tools on the left fender. The snap fastener, however, was an integral part of both fenders and was attached on the production line.

The pickaxe was held in place by a snap fastener on the right fender.

Unlike the Ausf C, Ausf D versions did not come with a rear view mirror on the front fender's right boom. Eliminating this mirror helped speed up production and saved on raw materials. The right front fender, however, had provisions for carrying a pickaxe. Also, the Ausf D was not equipped with the two high beam lights (one on each front fender) the Ausf C had. Instead, the left fender had a single Notek blackout light.

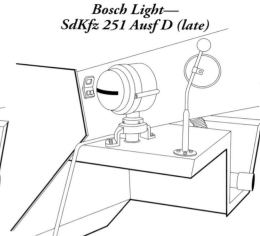

Light Development

Notek Blackout Light—
SdKfz 251 Ausf D (standard)

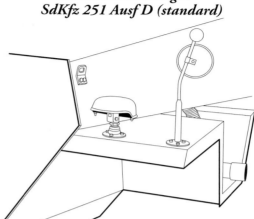

Bosch Light—
SdKfz 251 Ausf D (late)

The left boom did have a rear view mirror provided for the driver. Also, the Notek blackout light was attached to the left front fender, and the axe, when included, was held in place by a snap fastener.

Notek blackout light (left fender only) on standard SdKfz 151 Ausf D vehicles

Bosch light (left fender only) on late SdKfz Ausf D vehicles

Almost every Wehrmacht vehicle had a Notek blackout light. This light was built in large quantities by the Nova Technik factory at Munich, Bavaria. The driver could regulate the light's intensity, which had a 40-meter (length) by 25-meter (width) visibility range. This limited nighttime visibility reduced the vehicle's top speed to approximately 30 km/h.

Ausf D models had straight, front fenders. Additionally, standard production Ausf Ds had no position light on either fender, which on was placed between the Notek blackout light and the boom on Ausf Cs. However, early production SdKfz 251 Ausf D's did have a position light on the right fender.

11

This rare, front-bent right fender indicates an early production SdKfz 251 Ausf D.

The straight front fender, however, is the more common feature for Ausf Ds.

A few early production Ausf Ds did adopt the front fender configuration from the Ausf C model, but these bent fenders were a rarity. Standard production vehicles had straight fenders, which helped speed up the vehicle's assembly. Eliminating the standard Ausf C high beam lights from the top of the fender on the Ausf D also helped speed up vehicle production. No tools were attached on the upper surface of this featured fender, and this particular example even lacks the snap fastener for carrying tools.

Compared to early Ausf Ds that adopted the Ausf C's front fender, the lower plate connecting the front fender with the track fender was longer on standard production Ausf Ds. Additionally, the shape of the forward slanted fairing was altered and became a triangular shape.

All Ausf Ds had no exhaust muffler on the vehicle's right side. So, only the left side had a muffler. The thickness of the fender's edge, which protected the tracks, is the same its entire length on this early production vehicle.

As stated previously, very early production Ausf Ds used the Ausf C's front fender design. These early vehicles had shorter plates connecting the front fender with the track fender. The armor body's slanted fairing also was different from standard production models.

Placing the exhaust outlet on the upper part of the drum-shaped muffler gave the Ausf D a 50 cm fording depth. Four bolts secured the muffler to the connecting plate, and the standard muffler's design remained the same during the vehicle's production life.

The lower part of the muffler had a cylindrical pod shape.

The Ausf D only had a muffler on the left side, which was for the Maybach HL 42 TUKRRM 6-cylinder, water-cooled engine. The muffler fit into the lower plate that connected the the front fender to the the track fender. The connecting plate was longer on Ausf Ds than on previous sub-types such as the SdKfz 251 Ausf C. Though the mufflers were painted matte black during production, this muffler is rusted with age.

This shot features the upper part of the elliptical-shaped muffler on an early production vehicle.

These non-standard mufflers had exhaust outlets on the muffler's base, which reduced the vehicle's fording depth.

A few early production SdKfz 251 Ausf D vehicles had an elliptical-shaped muffler, which was a rarity on Ausf D models. Like standard production vehicles, however, the muffler was only on the half-track's left side. Also, this early design had a shorter plate connecting the front fender with the track fender than standard production vehicles.

A common feature on Ausf Ds was the white military license plate painted on the front armor plate, shown here on this SdKfz 251/7. The license plate is outlined in black. *WH* stands for Wehrmacht Heer (Army). No license numbers are painted on this particular license plate, but normally, SdKfz 251s did have painted-on license numbers.

The left front section view of the SdKfz 251/9 Ausf D shows the vehicle's synthetic rubber tire. The vast Buna Werk (Buna factory), owned by IG Farbenindustrie AG, produced most of the synthetic rubber. When the first SdKfz 251 Ausf D left the assembly line in 1943, German rubber was 94 percent synthetic. In 1944, 100 percent of the rubber produced was synthetic.

These armored doors gave acces to the Maybach HL 42 TUKRRM 6-cylinder, water-cooled engine. The Maybach engine rated 2,800 rpm (100 hp) and was gasoline powered. The Maybach motor company built luxury cars before WWII. The company was located at Friedrichshafen on Lake Constance but established a number of factories in the Third Reich that manufactured engines for the SdKfz 251 and most other German tanks.

In front of the Maybach HL 42 TUKRRM engine was a single engine oil cooler. The cooler's frame incorporated two fans. The Maybach power plant had a bore of 4,171 cc, and its compression ratio was 6.7-to-1. In front of the armored cover doors for the engine compartment is the armored cover for the circular radiator filler access.

This hinge is on the armored cover plate for the engine compartment. Two of these hinges were attached to each door on the front armored superstructure.

This view shows an outside look at the armored driver's compartment. A distinctive feature for the Ausf D is the visor slit on each side of the superstructure, which replaced the Ausf C's vision port and armored shield. This modification helped speed up production.

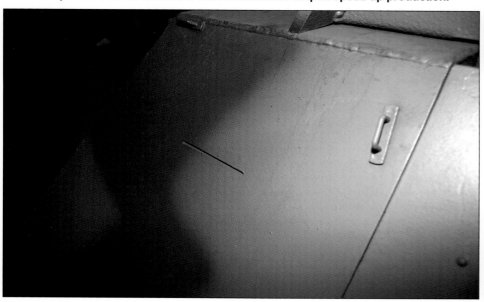

The armored cover doors had two locks located on the upper and lower part of the right armor plate. The locks were opened with a T-shaped-handle.

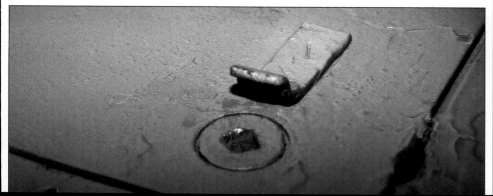

The Ausf D's right Panzergehäuse consisted of different armor panels welded to a single superstructure. The vehicle's sides had 8-mm thick armor protection. The Ausf D did not have the engine air intake cowls that the Ausf C had. Instead, the engine air intake was moved under the front armor cover.

The view looks at the left engine compartment of an SdKfz 251/9 Ausf D with a 7.5 cm KwK 37 L/24 gun. The vision port on the front surface of the crew compartment is open. This port is protected by an armored shield that could be lowered in combat.

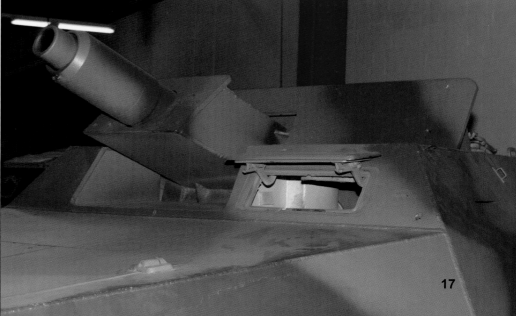

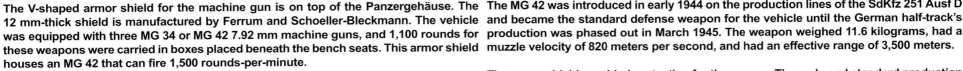

The V-shaped armor shield for the machine gun is on top of the Panzergehäuse. The 12 mm-thick shield is manufactured by Ferrum and Schoeller-Bleckmann. The vehicle was equipped with three MG 34 or MG 42 7.92 mm machine guns, and 1,100 rounds for these weapons were carried in boxes placed beneath the bench seats. This armor shield houses an MG 42 that can fire 1,500 rounds-per-minute.

The SdKfz 251/7 Ausf D carried two MG 42 machine guns and 4,800 rounds of 7.92 mm ammunition. The half-track's crew compartment is covered by canvas, a rarity. A special feature for the MG 42 was the fact that the barrel could be switched out in seconds. An MG 42's barrel had to be switched out after approximately 4,000 rounds were fired.

The MG 42 was introduced in early 1944 on the production lines of the SdKfz 251 Ausf D and became the standard defense weapon for the vehicle until the German half-track's production was phased out in March 1945. The weapon weighed 11.6 kilograms, had a muzzle velocity of 820 meters per second, and had an effective range of 3,500 meters.

The armor shield provided protection for the gunner. The early and standard production batches of the SdKfz 251 Ausf D were all equipped with an MG 34 7.92 mm machine gun, and the late production batches were all equipped with an MG 42 of the same caliber. This armor shield is part of a vehicle on exhibit at the Schweizerisches Militärmuseum (Swiss Military Museum) at Full, Switzerland.

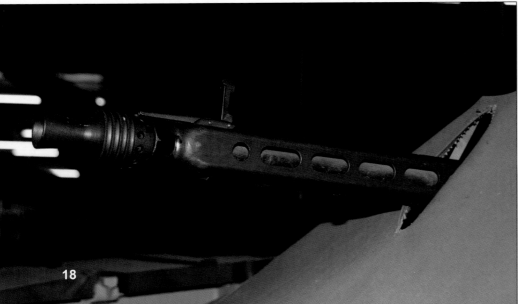

This retractable armor plate is on the left front vision port of an Ausf D. The armor shield was opened and retracted manually by a lever located inside the crew compartment.

This view shows the standard armor plate for the vision port of an SdKfz 251 Ausf D.

The armor plate for the left vision port had a slit cut into it. The left and right vision ports for the driver and commander, respectively, were identical.

This SdKfz 251 Ausf D has the early type of armor plate for the front vision ports.

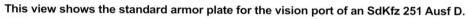

A windshield with built-in, manually operated wipers could be installed in the open vision ports to help protect the driver from dust, dirt, or rain.

A typical feature for the SdKfz 251 Ausf D were the three stowage bins built into the lower sides of the vehicle's Panzergehäuse. The body, welded from armor plates, was ballistically well-shaped.

Very early production SdKfz 251 Ausf Ds had only two stowage bins per side, as seen on this vehicle. The front stowage bin is the one that is missing.

The SdKfz 251 Ausf D's design was simplified, and many complicated features from previous models were eliminated to speed up production and to fulfill the German Wehrmacht's increasing need for this half-track. The Ausf D had a straight rear plate and simplified doors. Stowage bins were built into the lower sides of the Panzergehäuse. The vehicle featured here is unusual because it only has two stowage bins on each side of its superstructure. Most Ausf Ds had three stowage bins on each side. Car factories built the H kl 6p chassis, and specialized steel manufacturing facilities built the armor body. The specialized steel plants were the Deutsche Edelstahlwerke AG in Krefeld, the Böhmisch-Mährische Maschinenfabriken AG - Werk Maschinenfabrik in Lieben near Prague (now Liben, Czech Republic), the Schoeller-Bleckmann AG in Ternitz (Niederdonau), the Kesselfabrik L. & C. Steinmüller at Gummersbach near Cologne, and the Aktiengesellschaft Ferrum-Werk Laurahütte in Kattowitz at Silesia (now Katowice, Poland). The chassis and armor body were put together when final assembly took place at one of four assembly plants in the Third Reich—J. Gollnow & Sohn Eisen Konstruktionen at Stettin in Western Pomerania (now Szczecin, Poland), Hannoversche Maschinenbau AG (Hanomag) in Hannover-Linden, Eisenwerke Weserhütte AG in Bad Oeynhausen (Westfalen), or Waggon-und Maschinenbau AG (Wumag) in Görlitz. Adlerwerke in Frankfurt, Hanomag in Hannover, Auto Union in Zwickau, and Skodawerke in Pilsen (now Plzeň, Czech Republic) manufactured the Ausf D's automotive components. The hull sides had 8 mm-thick armor, and the Panzergehäuse protected its crew against small arms and artillery fragments. The roof for the crew, however, was not armored. The driver and the commander were the only ones protected by an armored roof.

The stowage bin was introduced on Ausf D variant. The armor plate's slant indicates this stowage bin is the right forward one. Very early production vehicles lacked front stowage bins and were equipped only with a center and rear stowage bin on each side of the superstructure.

The left stowage bin on this early SdKfz 251 Ausf D is located on the lower superstructure. A hinge is located on the base of the bin, and the door opens to the downward.

All six stowage bins were secured by locks attached to chains on the door in order to deter unauthorized borrowing of equipment that was stowed in the bins.

This view of the Ausf D's rear superstructure shows the rear fender, which had a painted-on license plate. All Ausf Ds had a license plate and number painted on the rear fender. Steel sheet-stamped license numbers were never used on these vehicles.

The armor body's lower rear end has a stepped-up shape. The armor plates on the lower chassis were 5.5 mm thick, which was less thick than the front or side armor.

The straight rear plate, a typical feature for the SdKfz 251 Ausf D, was one of many simplified designs that helped speed up vehicle production.

The tracked suspension consisted of 12 interleaved, pressed steel wheels with solid rubber tires (six wheels per side). To the front of the tracked suspension was the drive sprocket, and the rear idler was used for track tension control. The track itself was composed of ribbed steel castings, which had holes drilled in them for lightness. The inside track had a drive tooth. While the left track had 55 links, the right track had 56 links. Pins in lubricated needle bearings connected the tracks, and most Ausf Ds had hard rubber pads on the outside of the tracks. This particular example, however, has steel caps. A temporary shortage of sythetic rubber caused steel caps to be used briefly in summer 1944. These caps reduced the vehicle's top speed to 30 km/h. Higher speeds with steel caps on the tracks would have damaged the Ausf D's suspension components. Rubber pads on the track, however, were cleared by the Wehrmacht to allow the Ausf D a top speed of 52 km/h.

This view shows the left drive sprocket. Engine torque was transmitted from a Mercano PF 220 K dry twin-plate clutch to the mechanical transmission, which was located behind the differential. The brake-differential drive unit was based on a design developed by the Cleveland Tractor Company in Cleveland, Ohio, for its tracked tractors.

The SdKfz 251 Ausf D's left drive sprocket was identical to the one on the right side of the vehicle. Each sprocket was equipped with a drum brake. The driver used the brakes when the vehicle went up or down hills. Compressed air cylinders actuated the brakes by operating on the cables of mechanical self-servo brakes.

This drive sprocket is on the Ausf D's left side. A driving tooth on the inside of the track transferred power to the sprocket, which was equipped with rubber tires.

Early and standard production wheels typically had cover caps with two notches like this example on the left drive sprocket.

This view shows the spoke-shaped extensions of the left drive sprocket. Like the other wheels on the tracked suspension, the drive wheel was equipped with a rubber tire.

The wheel suspension arm was attached to the H kl 6p chassis frame. This device connected with the first twin wheel, which was behind the right drive sprocket.

This attachment connects the wheel suspension arm to the chassis. Each wheel pair was sprung with a transverse torsion bar.

Protected by a front fender, left drive sprockets of early and standard production SdKfz 251 Ausf Ds had a flat-surface cover cap with two notches. These notches were removed on late production SdKfz 251s, and the cover cap was changed to a rounded-surface with three rectangular metal sheets welded on its side.

The right drive sprocket of this SdKfz 251 Ausf D is visible with the drive tooth on the inside of the track.

The inner twin wheel was secured by a single outer wheel. The SdKfz 251 had steel-pressed wheels with solid rubber tires. Dunlop and Continental were the two German tire companies that manufactured the vehicle's tires.

Early and standard production Ausf Ds used this cover cap on the outer single wheel.

The cap on the inner twin wheel was used on early and standard production vehicles.

Late production SdKfz 251 Ausf Ds had three small metal pads welded around the side of the wheel cover cap with the rounded front surface, which was unlike standard production vehicles that had two notches in their cover caps with flat front surfaces.

SdKfz 251 Ausf D Standard and Late Development

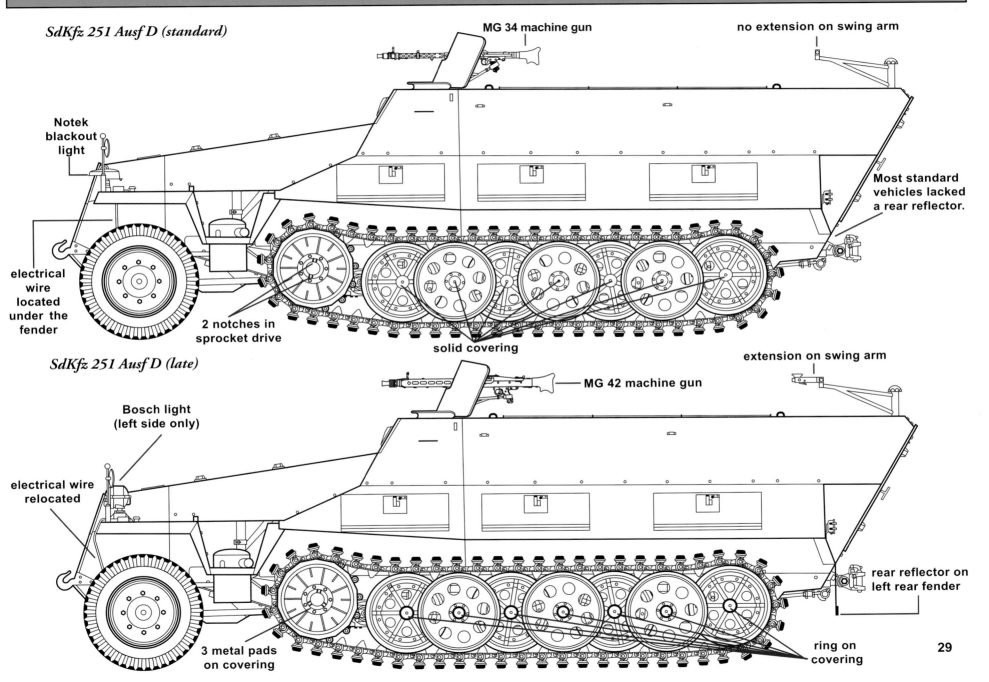

SdKfz 251 Ausf D (standard)

MG 34 machine gun

no extension on swing arm

Notek blackout light

Most standard vehicles lacked a rear reflector.

electrical wire located under the fender

2 notches in sprocket drive

solid covering

SdKfz 251 Ausf D (late)

extension on swing arm

Bosch light (left side only)

MG 42 machine gun

electrical wire relocated

rear reflector on left rear fender

3 metal pads on covering

ring on covering

29

This cover cap is on the driving sprocket of a late production Ausf D. The front surface is rounded, not flat like caps on standard production vehicless.

The later production SdKfz 251 Ausf D's cover cap for the inner twin wheel has an indented front surface and an outer metal ring surrounding that surface.

This late production SdKfz 251 Ausf D's outer single wheel has a cover cap with an indented front surface and a metal ring around that surface.

This view shows the tracked suspension of a late production SdKfz 251 Ausf D. These late vehicles had modified cover caps attached on the steel wheels.

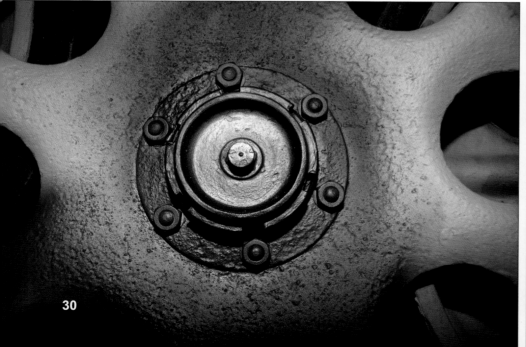

The outer twin wheel has stamped enforcement ribs, but the single outer wheel lacks these ribs.

Early and standard production vehicles used this outer single wheel cover cap.

This view shows an early production vehicle's tracked suspension. The inner twin wheels and outer single wheel have different shapes. The solid, synthetic rubber tires are 575/48 in dimension and 575 mm in diameter. All rubber tires were composed of Buna, a synthetic rubber. IG Farbenindustrie AG's vast Buna Werke (Buna factory) produced the majority of synthetic rubber. The huge plant started production in 1941 at Auschwitz (now O□wi□cim) near Kraców, Poland. The nearby Auschwitz-Birkenau concentration camp supplied forced labor for producing the tires.

31

The rear idler tensioned the track. The rubber-tired idler wheel has a diameter of 575 mm and is attached on a crank arm that is sprung by a torsion bar.

This view shows the idler tensioning device of an early production SdKfz 251 Ausf D. Armor plates mounted on the chassis' lower part protect the rear right torsion bar.

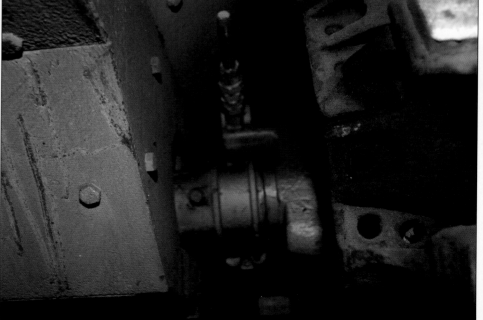

This view shows the left idler of an early production SdKfz 251 Ausf D. These tracks were equipped with steel caps, which reduced the vehicle's top speed to 30 km/h. At higher speeds, the steel shoes often vibrated loose and got lost. Most Ausf D tracks were equipped with rubber pads rather than steel pads.

The right idler on this vehicle has steel caps attached to the track. These caps are not a feature commonly found on early and standard production SdKfz 251 Ausf Ds. Most vehicles had rubber pads.

This type of idler was mounted on early and standard production SdKfz 251 Ausf Ds. These idlers had a flush-shaped cover cap.

This link forms part of the left track and has metal caps, which were unusual for these vehicles. After a brief period in summer 1944, metal caps where phased out.

This idler cover cap was a usual feature on early and standard production SdKfz 251s. The cap has a raised inner circular area. Late production cover caps had an indented front surface and an outer metal ring around that surface.

The rear tracked suspension on this late production SdKfz 251 Ausf D also shows the track with its hard rubber pads, which were standard on most Ausf Ds.

The late production SdKfz 251 Ausf Ds was equipped with hard rubber pads and had a top speed of 52 km/h, 22 km/h more than the Ausf Ds with steel caps.

This view shows the right idler of a late production SdKfz 251 Ausf D. Like all other wheels of the tracked suspension, the idler has a rubber tire.

This cover cap on the right idler of a late production Ausf D has an indented front surface and a metal ring that distinguishes it from caps on standard production vehicles.

The crew compartment exposed the crew from up top, but this SdKfz 251/7, on display at the Deutsches Panzermuseum at Munster, had a canvas cover for the crew compartment, which was a rarely used. The driver sat on the left-hand seat, and the commander sat to the driver's right. Two benches ran the length of the vehicle on each side and provided room for ten Panzergrenadiere (armored infantry soldiers). At the top of the armored cover for the the driver and the commander was an MG 42 7.92 mm machine gun mounted on a V-shaped armor shield.

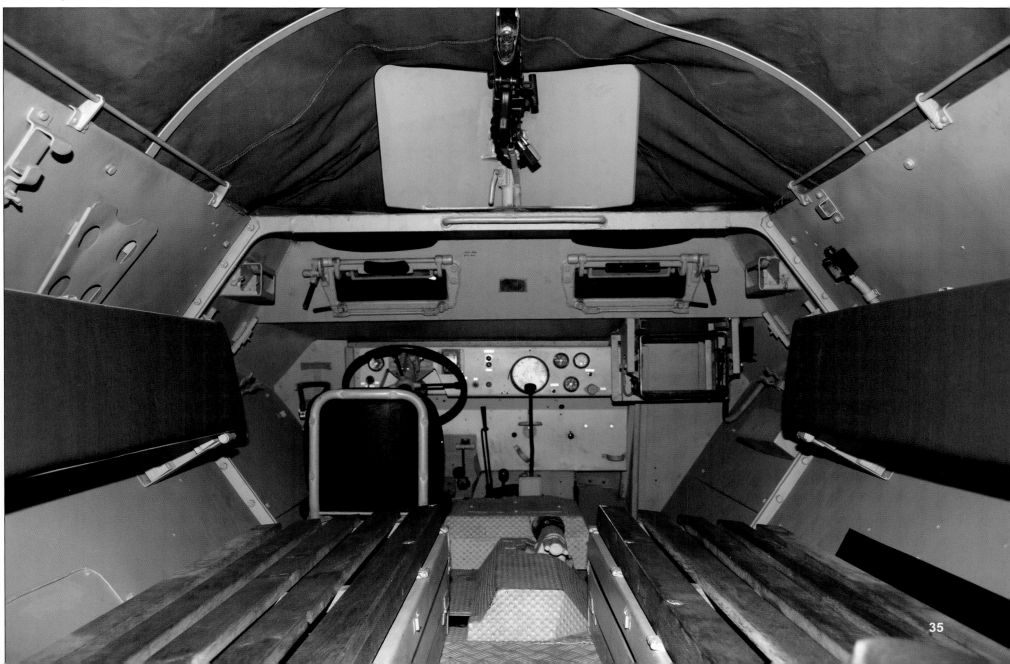

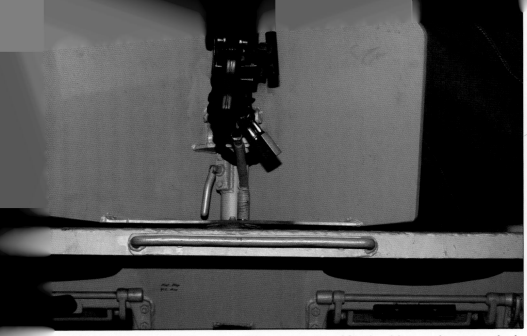

The V-shaped armor shield on top of the armored roof for the driver and commander is 2 mm thick. A handle is welded on the edge of the upper armor protection. The armor plate forms the roof of the vehicle and is 5.5 mm thick.

This view shows the lower part of the armor shield. The shield could be removed from the roof, if necessary.

This vehicle is armed with an MG 42. The body was made from cold pressed sheets of metal that were riveted together. The rear part of the gun and the grip were made from plastic. This design allowed for faster production. During WWII, 750,000 MG 42s were built by a number of factories, including Mauser and Steyr-Daimler-Puch.

These illustrations show the armor shield used for the MG 42 from 1944-1945.

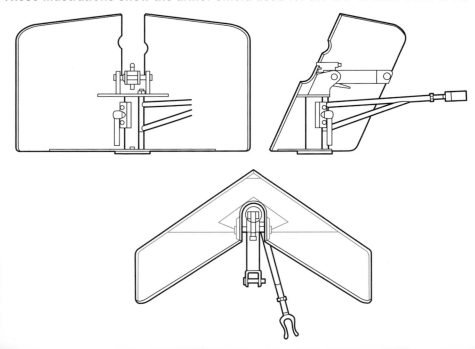

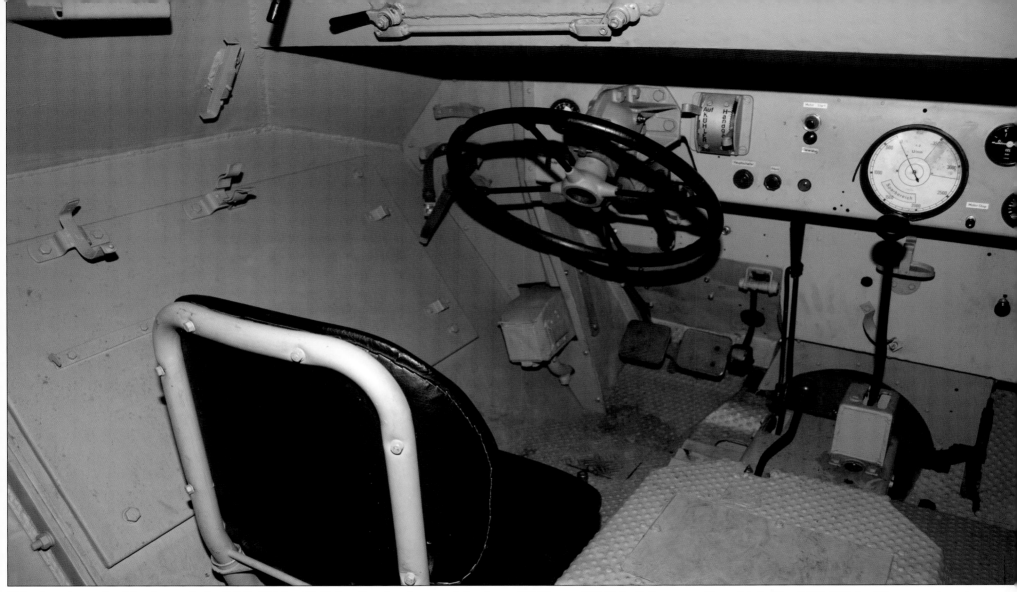

This view shows the driver's area in the SdKfz 251 Ausf D. Below the visor is a provision for an MP 38 or an MP 40, both 9 mm machine pistols. The SdKfz 251 Ausf D was equipped with two MG 34 7.92 mm machine guns and had provisions for two MP 38s or MP 40s to be stored in racks. Later production models had provisions for three MG 42 7.92 mm machine guns but only a single provision for one MP 38 or MP 40. All Ausf D models had a steering wheel mounted at an inverted angle to save space. This particular model, however, lacked the U-shaped tube that served as an air intake from the crew compartment to the Maybach engine. This U-shaped tube was standard on almost all Ausf Ds. The tachometer is located in the middle of the dashboard. The speedometer is missing. No Ausf D had a speedometer since the German Army was not concerned about speed limits in occupied territories. The large fairing on the floor is the covering for the gearbox. Also on the floor is a lever for the reduction gear control (red-knobbed lever), for the hand brake (black lever to red-knobbed lever's left), and for shifting gears (black-knobbed lever to the red-knobbed lever's right). The SdKfz 251 Ausf D had four forward speeds and one reverse speed. The reduction gearbox had high and low ratios. Thus, the number of speeds was doubled to eight forward and two reverse. To the left of the levers are three pedals. From right to left are the throttle (the small, black pedal with worn yellow paint), the clutch, and the brakes.

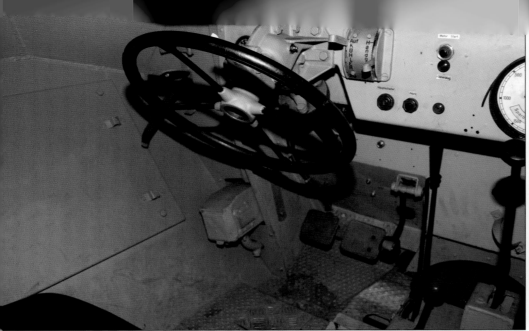

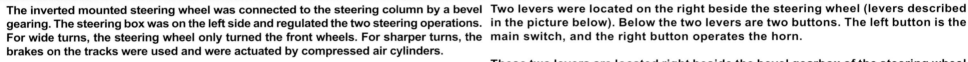

The inverted mounted steering wheel was connected to the steering column by a bevel gearing. The steering box was on the left side and regulated the two steering operations. For wide turns, the steering wheel only turned the front wheels. For sharper turns, the brakes on the tracks were used and were actuated by compressed air cylinders.

The red pointer is the position indicator, a feature introduced on all SdKfz 251 variants.

Two levers were located on the right beside the steering wheel (levers described in the picture below). Below the two levers are two buttons. The left button is the main switch, and the right button operates the horn.

These two levers are located right beside the bevel gearbox of the steering wheel and regulate the radiator (left lever) and the radiator flap (right lever).

The spartan dashboard of the SdKfz 251 Ausf D includes the two levers (next to the steering wheel) that regulated the radiator and the radiator flap and the buttons for the main switch and the horn. Prominent is the tachometer in the center of the dashboard. To the lower right of the tachometer is a single button that stops the engine. Next to these items are three instrument controls (described in the bottom right photo) and a button for instrument illumination.

The tachometer has a range between 380 and 3,500 revolutions per minute. *Sparbereich* stands for economic driving. The red area in the tachometer shows the driver when the vehicle has reached the critical engine revolution range, which could damage the powerplant.

The left upper instrument control shows oil pressure, and the right one shows the radiator's water temperature. The single lower instrument shows air pressure for the air servo assisted main brakes. The air compressor was mounted on the side of the engine, and the air tanks were placed under the chassis.

The fairing for the gearbox is located between the driver and the commander.

The gear-shift gearbox was located on the right, behind the fairing for the gearbox.

The gearbox and the engine reduction gearbox were covered by a fairing in the crew compartment. An access hatch is located on top of this covering.

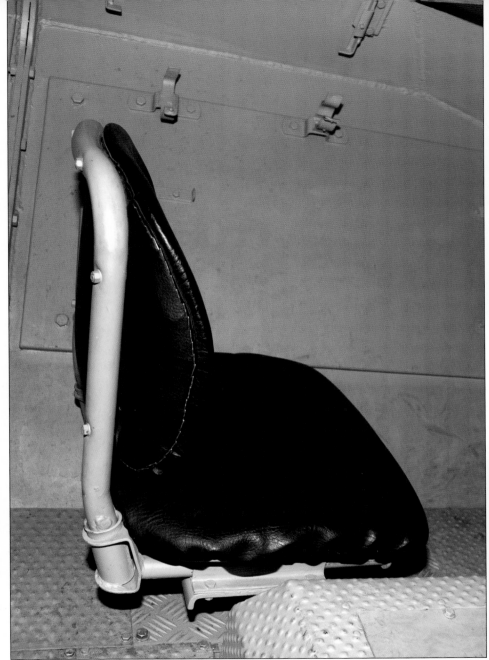

The driver's seat is covered in black leather. Leather color for seats varied by manufacturer. Sand or brown-red also were colors for the leather seats. Both seats have flip-up bases and could be removed. This vehicle used the same seats for the driver and the commander that were used in the German Panzerkampfwagen (tanks).

This device is a heater that thawed tubes connected to the cooling cycle of the engine and was a necessity for winter operation when temperatures could reach -30 degrees in areas where the Ausf D was stationed. The heater is located on the base of the left side armor. The curved tube below the heater directly leads to the engine compartment.

This view is of the left, armored roof. Only the driver and commander had an armored roof. A leather-covered cushion hangs from the roof. Just above the steering wheel is the visor. A small side visor is located on the inner side armor.

The front of the driver's compartment was protected by a 14.5 mm thick armor plate. This armor protection greatly reduced the angle of view for the driver and the commander. The visors were virtually unchanged through the Ausf D's production cycle.

The right visor for the commander provided the crew with a limited angle of view, which was further reduced when the armor was released for protection. The armor allowed a frontal view through a horizontal slit.

The left visor had a lever attached on the left that opened and closed the armor. The lower lever manually operated the windshield wiper, which was incorporated on a windshield that could be installed in the open visors to protect the driver and the commander against wind, dust, and rain. The windshield is not installed on this particular vehicle.

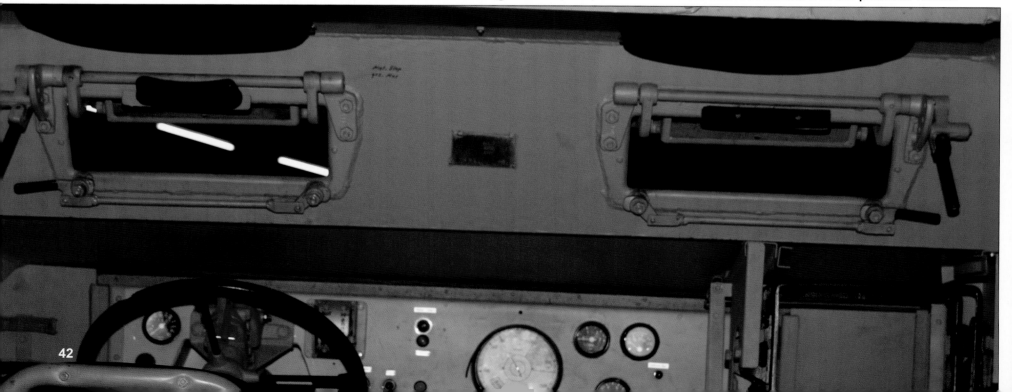
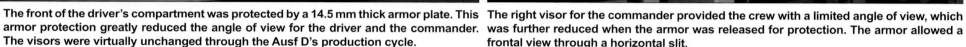

In the commander's compartment and beside the front visor is the side visor. Below the front visor is the frame for the radio. The frame was added during final vehicle assembly, but most vehicles lacked a radio. If a radio was carried, an antenna had to be carried. The antenna was fixed in an antenna socket on the armor body's upper edge.

In most cases, the frame for the radio set was installed only in the platoon leader's vehicle since most vehicles lacked radios. The radio allowed communication with command posts in the rear as well as other tanks. Behind the frame for the radio is the first aid kit. The cable connects the radio set with the antenna socket, located on the edge of the upper superstructure. Although the radio was fitted in few vehicles, the connecting cable was attached on the inner armor frame of all SdKfz 251s.

This frame carried the armor glass block, but the armor glass is missing here. The Ausf D carried several spare armor glass blocks that replaced damaged armor glass. In the inner armor protection is the slit that provides the commander with a limited side view. The Ausf D was the first variant equipped with slits. The Ausf D replaced the Ausf C's side visors with this vision slit to speed up the armor body's production.

Below the armored glass frame (barely visible in top right of photo) is a holder for the windshield, which inserted into the visor. The windshield, however, is missing here. The windshield was only used when no enemy action was expected since the armor plate could not retract with the windshield in place. Below the windshield holder is a rack for the MP 38 or MP 40 9 mm machine pistol. The right seat back is flipped up.

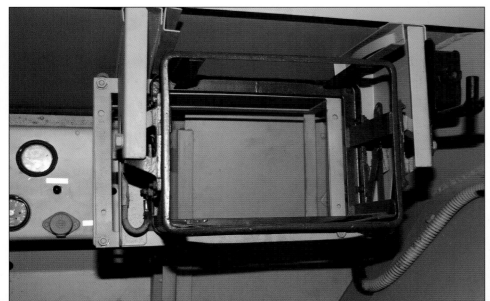

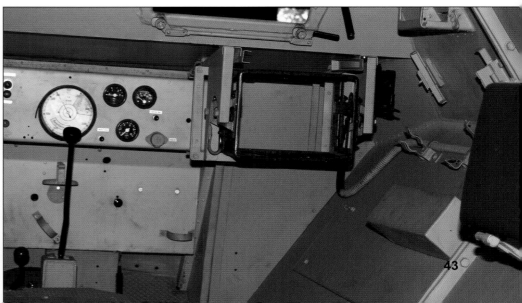

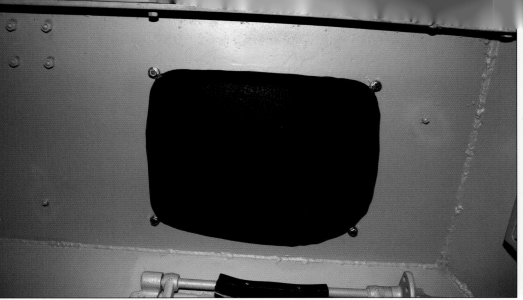

This cushion protected the commander's head. Leather covered this cushion, and screws secured it to the roof.

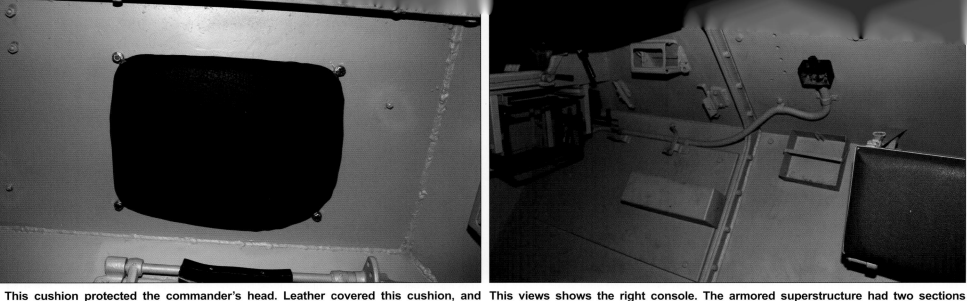

This views shows the right console. The armored superstructure had two sections bolted together behind the driving compartment. The bolts are visible here. The frame just in front of the leather-covered benches held spare armor glass blocks that could be inserted in the frame in front of the side slit. The cable attached on the inner armor plate connected the radio with the antenna socket, mounted on the edge of the upper superstructure. The antenna socket and antenna mast were only carried when a radio was built into the half-track.

This floor shows the floor viewed from the commander's position.

Antenna socket (Right side only)

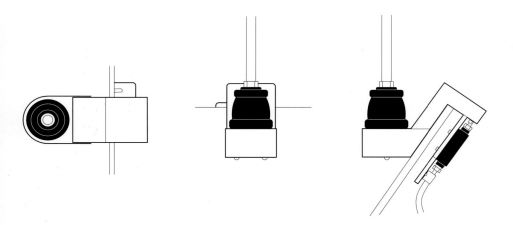

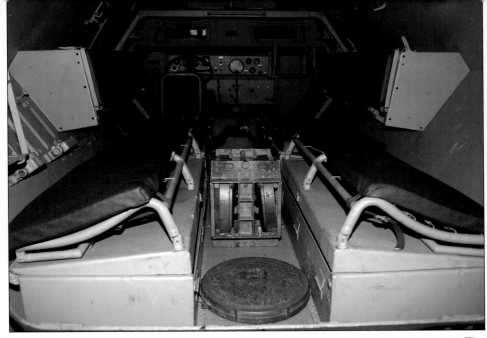

Two leather-covered benches were placed on each side of the crew compartment. The benches located to the rear of the crew compartment stowed ammunition boxes for the crew.

The pair of benches, located closest to the drivers compartment, were constructed out of wood. The benches had a leather-covered backrest that also served as a compartment for four rifles.

This bench also served as an ammunition stowage box for the MG 34 or MG 43 7.92 mm machine gun. Each bench could hold 10 boxes of ammunition.

The wooden benches could be adjusted two ways—the lower transport position and the higher combat position. The Panzergrenadiere (armored infantrymen) exited the SdKfz 251 during combat by jumping from the benches over the armored superstructure. The exit through the back doors was never used during training or actual combat.

Typical SdKfz 251/7 engineer vehicles had a frame attached to the rear, on the left side of the crew compartment. Standard production SdKfz 251/1s did not have this frame.

A spare window holder is attached above the left backrest on the upper slanted superstructure of this vehicle.

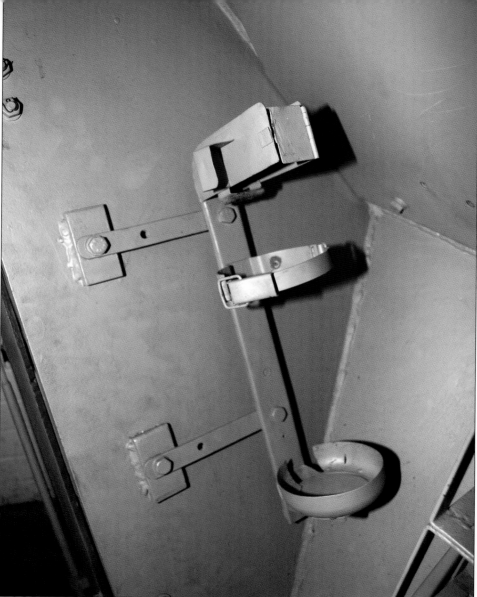

The holder, in the center right of this photo, is attached to the rear inner armor and housed a fire extinguisher. The fire extinguisher is not mounted on this SdKfz 251/7. Usually, the fire extinguisher was secured in its holder with a leather belt. The fire extinguisher holder was attached only on the left side of the vehicle. The position of the fire extinguisher is unique for the SdKfz 251/7 pioneer vehicle. The standard SdKfz 251/1 troop carrier had the fire extinguisher mounted on the right rear armor plate. The Ausf D and Ausf C were the only versions equipped with a fire extinguisher in the crew compartment. Earlier vehicle versions had the fire extinguisher placed on the vehicle's outer superstructure.

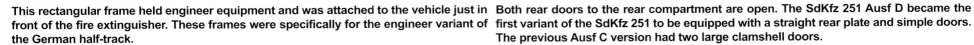

The rectangular frame, located on the rear cabin compartment, was a unique feature for the SdKfz 251/7 Ausf D.

This rectangular frame held engineer equipment and was attached to the vehicle just in front of the fire extinguisher. These frames were specifically for the engineer variant of the German half-track.

Two frames for engineer equipment were located close to the left bench on the SdKfz 251/7. These frames were not carried in the SdKfz 251/1, troop carrrier version.

Both rear doors to the rear compartment are open. The SdKfz 251 Ausf D became the first variant of the SdKfz 251 to be equipped with a straight rear plate and simple doors. The previous Ausf C version had two large clamshell doors.

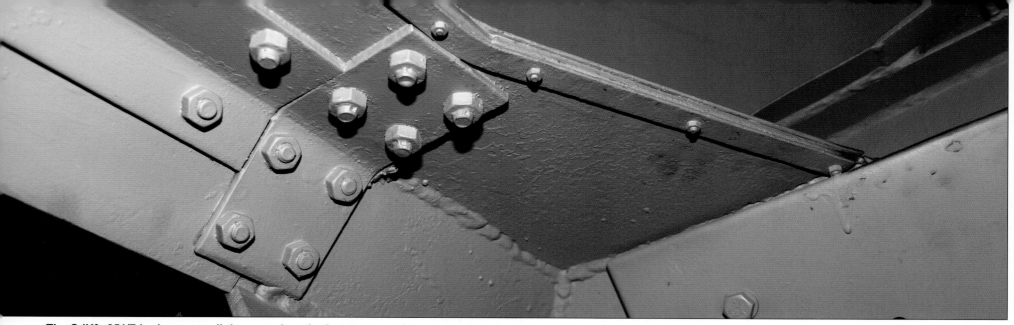

The SdKfz 251/7 had screws, all the same length, that connected the upper door frame with the superstructure of the half-track. This particular SdKfz 251/7 had a metal ledge attached to the edge of the superstructure. This ledge was not featured in the SdKfz 251/9 Ausf D, exhibited in the Deutsches Panzermuseum.

Removing the screws allowed removal of the upper door frame. The screws in this vehicular example are different lengths, which was uncommon. The metal plate welded on the inner armor plate also is an uncommon feature for the SdKfz 251 Ausf D half-track.

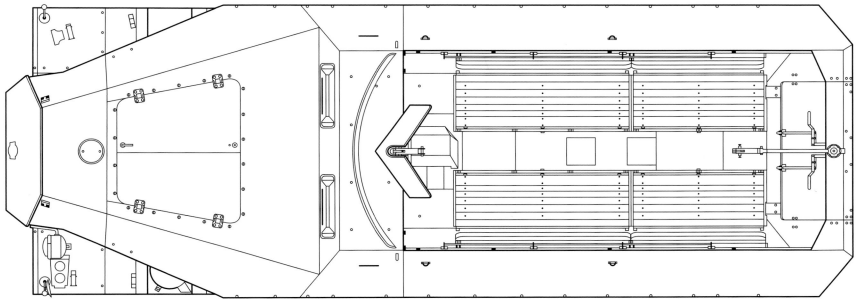

Specifications

- Length: 5.8 meters
- Width: 2.1 meters
- Height: 1.75 meters
- Weight (Loaded): 8.5 metric tons

- Powerplant: Maybach HL 42 TUKRRM six-cylinder, water-cooled, 100 hp
- Transmission: 4-speed, mechanical, Mercano PF 220 K clutch
- Speed: 52 km/h (road), 30 km/h (off-road)
- Range: 300 km (road), 150 km (cross country)
- Armament: 2 MG 42 7.92 mm machine guns
- Crew: 12

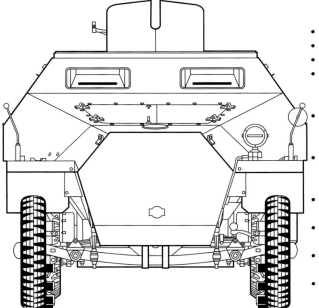

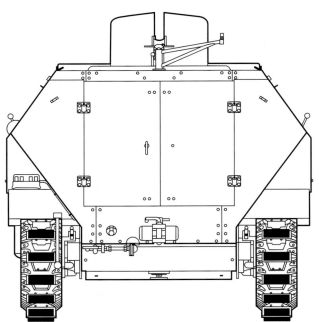

SdKfz 251/9 Ausf D Very Early and Standard Development

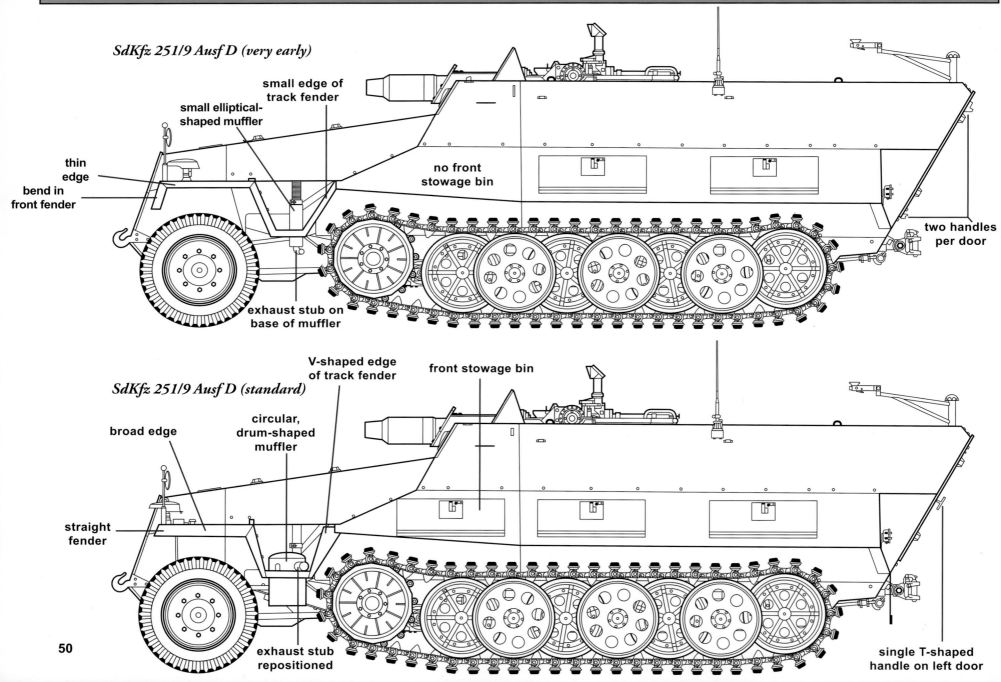

SdKfz 251/9 Ausf D (very early)

small edge of
track fender

small elliptical-
shaped muffler

thin
edge

bend in
front fender

no front
stowage bin

two handles
per door

exhaust stub on
base of muffler

V-shaped edge
of track fender

front stowage bin

SdKfz 251/9 Ausf D (standard)

circular,
drum-shaped
muffler

broad edge

straight
fender

exhaust stub
repositioned

single T-shaped
handle on left door

50

The SdKfz 251 Ausf D was the first German half-track variant equipped with simple doors. Each manufactured door was a 5.5 mm-thick armor plate. The Panzergrenadiere (armored infantry) boarded the vehicle through the rear doors. However, during combat or exercises, the soldiers exited the half-track by jumping over the superstructure.

Very early examples of the SdKfz 251 Ausf D had a non-standard release mechanism on the two rear doors. Handles fixed on the top and bottom ends of the outer surfaces of the doors rotated latches on the inside. Subsequent production batches of the SdKfz 251 Ausf D eliminated these handles and replaced them with a rod design.

On standard production Ausf Ds, a rod system on the inside opened and closed the doors when a crewmember used the attached handle. This rod system replaced the early handles and latches that only could be opened from outside.

The open rear right door of this very early Ausf D shows the two hinges on the inner and outer surface end plate that were used on both the right and left rear doors. The slanted end plate became a dedicated feature for the SdKfz 251 Ausf D.

This view shows the upper, outer handle on the right rear door of a very early SdKfz 251 Ausf D. Upper handles were mounted vertically their respective rear door.

This view shows the lower, outer handle on the right rear door. This handle was mounted on only the very first Ausf Ds, which were equipped with simple rear doors. The lower handles were mounted horizontally on the rear doors.

This view shows the left, rear entrance door's lower, inner fastener on a very early production Ausf D. Turning the upper and lower fasteners allowed the doors to open.

The early production SdKfz 251 Ausf D's upper, inner fastener was shorter than the lower, inner fastener.

Early production German half-track vehicles lacked the rod-shaped opening mechanism that was a typical feature on standard production Ausf Ds. The rear doors could not be opened from inside, which made exiting through the rear doors impossible.

Each standard production SdKfz 251 Ausf D door was equipped with this door handle. Opening or closing the door simply required a pull or push of the handle.

The opening mechanism returned to the locked position with the help of a spring attached on the upper U-shaped guide on the inner surface of the armored rear door. Each inner door surface had a retracting spring.

A rod system was introduced on the standard production SdKfz 251 Ausf D to facilitate opening and closing the rear armored dorrs. The system's biggest advance allowed the crew to open and close the doors from inside the crew compartment. To operate the doors, a crew member used a single handle, which was located on the inner surface of either door. With the new handle and rod system, the small fasteners on the upper and lower surfaces were deleted from the Ausf D.

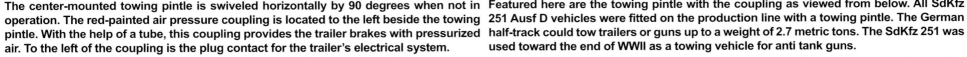

The rod's U-shaped guide was attached to the lower, inner surface of the armored rear door on both the left and right doors.

The center-mounted towing pintle is swiveled horizontally by 90 degrees when not in operation. The red-painted air pressure coupling is located to the left beside the towing pintle. With the help of a tube, this coupling provides the trailer brakes with pressurized air. To the left of the coupling is the plug contact for the trailer's electrical system.

The upper hinge was secured with four bolts on the inner surface of the rear plate and the door. Two hinges were attached for each door.

Featured here are the towing pintle with the coupling as viewed from below. All SdKfz 251 Ausf D vehicles were fitted on the production line with a towing pintle. The German half-track could tow trailers or guns up to a weight of 2.7 metric tons. The SdKfz 251 was used toward the end of WWII as a towing vehicle for anti tank guns.

The pivoting machine gun mount is attached on the upper rear superstructure with a stud and accommodates an MG 34 or an MG 42 7.92 mm machine gun.

The pivoting machine gun mount was attached on a pin. Bolts secured the pin to the upper superstructure's connecting frame. The mount could be removed from the pin, and a number of crews removed the device when the machine gun was not mounted.

The right rear fender on an early production Ausf D was welded on the rear lower superstructure. The vehicle had a much steeper angle on the rear fender than previous versions of the half-track. The license number was painted on the left fender only. Only a few vehicles had license numbers painted on the right rear fender as well.

SdKfz 251 Ausf D License Plate Development

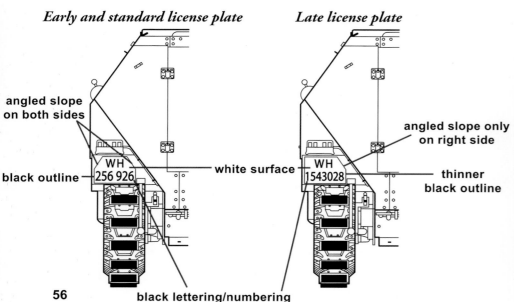

Early and standard license plate

Late license plate

angled slope on both sides

angled slope only on right side

black outline

white surface

WH 256 926

WH 1543028

thinner black outline

black lettering/numbering

The four green lights on the Notek Abstandsrückleuchte (convoy tail light) helped drivers keep the necessary distance while driving in convoys. If the driver kept the correct distance during night driving, he saw two green lights. Four green lights meant the driver was too close behind the preceding vehicle, and a single green light meant the driver was too far away from the preceding vehicle in a convoy. The Notek Abstandsrückleuchte was used during operations near the front or where the enemy was expected. The metal sheet covered the lower two lights.

By flipping the metal cover up, the Notek light mode could be changed. The left red light was the tail light, and the right orange light was the stop light. These two light settings were used when no enemy action was expected. The Notek Abstandsrückleuchte was manufactured by the German Nova Technik company at Munich in Bavaria.

Early and standard production vehicles had upper angled slopes on both sides of the license plate. Late production vehicles had an upper angled slope on the right edge only. All Ausf Ds had the license plate painted directly on the front armor plate and the rear fender. The license numbers on this example were painted in a white square and outlined in black. Since the SdKfz 251 traveled on ordinary roads, the Wehrmacht allocated license plate numbers to them. The letters WH stand for Wehrmacht Heer (German Army).

Above the license plate is the Notek Abstandsrückleuchte (convoy tail light). This light was mounted on only the left tail of all SdKfz 251 variants. The Notek became the principal convoy tail light of the Wehrmacht and was mounted on almost all German tanks, half-tracks, or trucks.

This SdKfz 251/9 Ausf D, on exhibit in the Deutsches Panzermuseum in Munster, Germany; is a very early example of the 7.5 cm cannon-equipped half-track. This variant was a close support vehicle with heavy firepower and was developed from the standard SdKfz 251/1 armored personnel carrier. The Panzergrenadiere (armored infantry) needed heavy firepower, a need fully tracked assault gun units could not fulfill. This KwK 37 L/24 7.5 cm gun was located in the crew compartment. The weapon was mounted on a pedestal supported by the vehicle's frame. The front plate above the right crew position was cut out for the KwK 37 L/24 gun, which had a traverse of 12 degrees to the right and 10 degrees to the left. The elevation arc was limited to -5 to +20 degrees. The vehicle carried 52 rounds in the crew compartment. The gun raised the vehicle's combat weight to 8,650 kilograms. Beside the KwK 37 L/24 gun, the half-track was equipped with a single MG 34 7.92 mm machine gun and an MP 38 9 mm machine pistol. The driver, commander, and gunner made up the crew. Production of this Ausf D variant lasted from March 1943 to December 1943. Approximately 630 examples were produced before production was switched to the SdKfz 251/9 with the Kanone 51.The half-track had non-standard front fenders that were bent at the front and the non-standard elliptical-shaped muffler with the exhaust stub on the base of the muffler. In contrast to the standard production SdKfz 251 Ausf Ds with three stowage bins, this particular unit only had two stowage bins on the lower superstructure. This displayed vehicle is one of very few gun-equipped variants that exist in the world today.

The KwK 37 L/24 gun was offset to the right in the close support SdKfz 251/9. The front plate is cut to make room for the 7.5 cm gun and its shield.

This view shows details of the KwK 37 L/24 gun muzzle. The barrel's inner surface is rifled to put a spin on the shells it fires and to increase target accuracy. The short barrel is responsible for the weapon's lower muzzle velocity.

The offset mounted KwK 37 L/24 gun is located on an SdKfz 251/9 Ausf D. The barrel is protected by a shield. Due to the cut in the right front plate, the commander's visor was removed, but the driver's visor remained. The observation slit on the right side of the superstructure also was removed, however, the vision slit on the left side of the superstructure, which was standard on all SdKfz 251/1 troop carriers, remained. Additionally, the forward stowage bin was removed. The KwK 37 L/24 gun mounting did not appreciably heighten the vehicle's silhouette.

The 7.5 cm gun was incorporated into the front structure of the SdKfz 251/9. The commander's visor was removed to compensate for the gun's placement. The visor for the driver, however, remained on this Ausf D variant.

The roof on the right superstructure has the shield added around the 7.5 cm gun. Evident is the removal of side vision slit for the commander, which was a design feature of the close support variant Ausf D.

The armor shield was added on top of the KwK 37 L/24 gun and was attached on top of the vehicle's front shield. A single, triangular gusset was attached to the inner frame and the left-side of the roof. To the right, two triangular gussets were welded on the roof. This armor shield protected the gunner and loader against small arms fire from the front.

The KwK 37 L/24 gun had a short barrel and got the nickname *Stummel* (stub) from Wehrmacht soldiers.

The KwK 37 L/24 gun was offset to the right. Most of these 7.5 cm short barrel weapons previously saw service with the Panzerkampfwagen IV (PzKpfw IV for short) and were left over when the standard German Wehrmacht tanks were upgraded with the long barreled KwK 40 gun of the same caliber.

The hand wheel located on the KwK 37 L/24 gun's left breech was for setting the elevation. The hand wheel below traversed the gun. This particular SdKfz 251/9 lacks the Sfl. Z.F.1 gunsight, which usually was mounted on the rear slanted boom above the wheel. The Sfl. Z.F. 1 was used during direct fire against enemy targets.

This view shows the KwK 37 L/24 gun mounted on its recoil guard, which was modified so the loader had to be seated. Only the left side of the recoil guard had solid protection. This metal plate was attached on the two U-shaped tubes that formed the recoil guard.

The hand wheels were used to properly set the KwK 37 L/24 gun elevation. The cannon had a traverse of 12 degrees to the right and 10 degrees to the left. The elevation and traverse mechanism was directly taken from the Panzerkampfwagen IV, in which the gun previously saw action.

(Top) This view shows the KwK 37 L/24 installation in the crew compartment as seen from the open rear doors of the SdKfz 251/9. Evident are the sheets on the roof that covered the pedestal for the KwK 37 L/24 gun. The V-shaped frame on the left and right inner armored superstructure is the place where the vehicle's forward and rear superstructure were bolted together. A seat was mounted for the gunner on the left side of the cannon. All the benches and backrests were removed from this gun-equipped vehicle. This Ausf D variant carried 52 rounds of ammunition, which were stored in the crew compartment. The ammunition load consisted of high explosive shells, armor piercing shells, and smoke shells. These shells had a range of approximately 6,000 meters.

(Bottom Left) The KwK 37 L/24 gun was mounted on a pedestal supported by the vehicle frame. This pedestal was covered by sheets of steel in the rear crew compartment.

(Bottom Right) This view shows the SdKfz 251/9's driver compartment. This particular vehicle has the inverted U-shaped tube that served as the air intake from the crew compartment to the Maybach engine. The tube is attached to the bulkhead. Most Ausf Ds were equipped with this air intake. The commander's seat was eliminated in this close support variant.

The recoil guard for the KwK 37 L/24 gun is right of the centerline in the crew compartment. The recoil guard was altered so the gunner was seated while loading the gun.

The gunner's seat was mounted on the cannon breech's extensions. The top hand wheel, located to the left of the gun, was for gun elevation while the bottom hand wheel was for gun traverse. The boom shaped extension beside the left hand wheel usually housed the Sfl. Z.F. 1 periscope gunsight, but this device is not mounted on this vehicle.

This view shows the upper part of the KwK 37 L/24 gun with the armor shield on the rear. The armor shield was welded to the vehicle superstructure, and a smaller shield was mounted on the gun barrel. Note the two triangular gussets on the shield's right side.

The left side of the recoil guard was attached to the breech of the KwK 37 L/24 gun. Early Ausf Cs had a bath tub-shaped covering as a recoil guard, but the Ausf D had two parallel tubes as a guard, which saved on German raw materials.

This view shows the left side of the recoil guard for the KwK 37 L/24 gun. The gun's breech mechanism is visible. The 7.5 cm gun allowed the SdKfz 251/9 to engage enemy strong points, but its weak armor made the half-track less suited to a role as a tank destroyer despite its ability to fire armor piercing shells.

This view shows the upper breech of the KwK 37 L/24 gun. Visible toward the back of the photograph is the elevation mechanism for the gun.

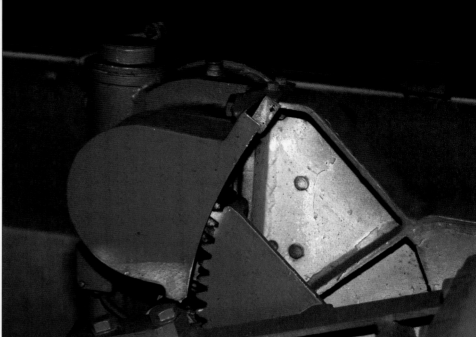

The small shield was attached on the upper portion of the barrel and moved with the gun. Left of the barrel is the elevation mechanism for the KwK 37 L/24 gun.

This view shows the elevation mechanism. The hand wheels worked on a tooth that regulated the gun's proper elevation. This mechanism was to the left of the gun barrel.

The SdKfz 251/9 had its right access door on the rear stowage bin faired over. This particular vehicle is non-standard because it only had provision for two stowage bins on each side of the superstructure instead of three.

This view looks at the faired over access door for the rear right stowage bin on the SdKfz 251/9. Unlike the right stowage bin, the left, rear stowage bin remained on the superstructure of the vehicle.

Instead of the headrest that was found on the SdKfz 251/1, the SdKfz 251/9 had a container located on the right inner surface of the vehicle's crew compartment.

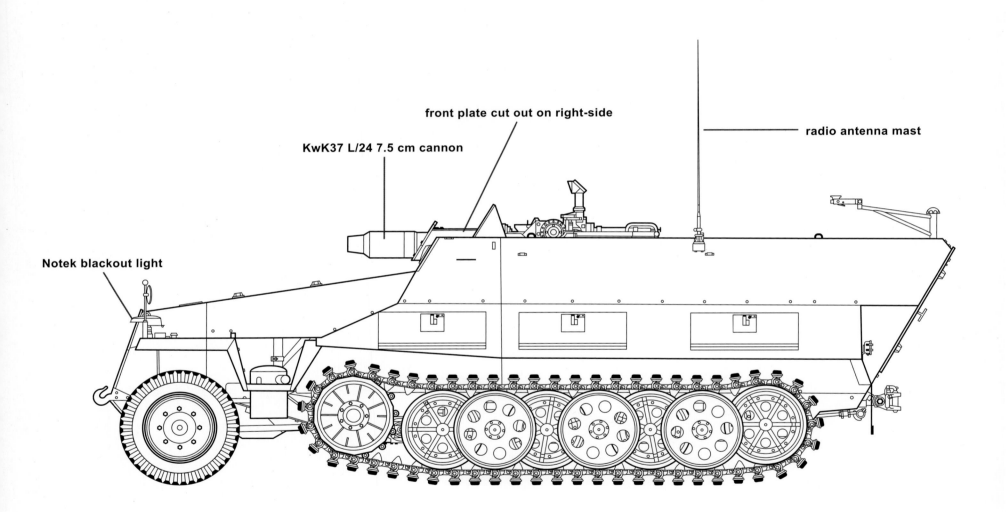

front plate cut out on right-side

KwK37 L/24 7.5 cm cannon

radio antenna mast

Notek blackout light

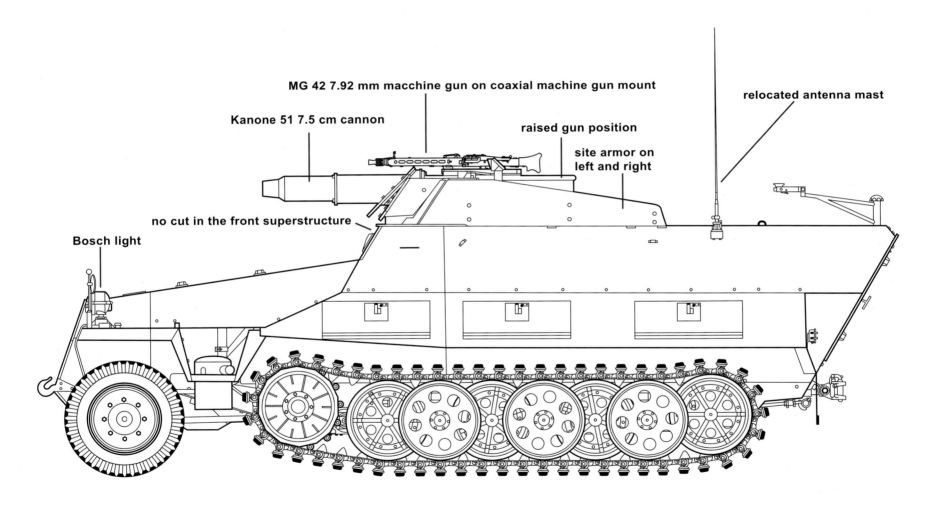

MG 42 7.92 mm macchine gun on coaxial machine gun mount

Kanone 51 7.5 cm cannon

raised gun position

relocated antenna mast

site armor on left and right

no cut in the front superstructure

Bosch light

The SdKfz 251/7 Ausf D Mittlerer Pionierpanzerwagen (medium engineer vehicle) was a derivative of the SdKfz 251/1 troop carrier. The vehicle's main mission was to support the German tank brigade on the battlefield, and the half-track carried combat engineer equipment, bridge layer equipment, and explosive charges. Additional engineering equipment was carried inside the vehicle. The equipment included various types of mines, explosive charges, and mine detectors. Two support brackets were attached on each side of the upper superstructure. These brackets carried two Übergangsschienen 8 (8 metric ton assault bridges), which were used to bridge trenches or large shell holes. The assault bridges were distinctive features for the SdKfz 251/7 Ausf D. This particular example, on exhibit in the Deutsches Panzermuseum at Munster, has wooden planking inserted between its support brackets. Only a small number of SdKfz 251/7 Ausf Ds used wooden planking. A combat-loaded vehicle weighed 8,870 kilograms. The SdKfz 251/7 Ausf D had a crew of seven or eight soldiers and was armed with two MG 42 7.92 mm machine guns and 4,800 rounds. This vehicle also has the crew compartment covered with canvas, a feature rarely seen in combat during WWII.

This view shows the right front support bracket of an SdKfz 251/7 Ausf D. The support brackets were bolted against the upper superstructure of the German half-track. The bracket's metal profiles were made from metal pieces that were welded together. All support brackets had a circular aperture in the front face. Atop the support bracket is a single Übergangsschiene 8.

The two Übergangsschienen 8 were a typical feature of the SdKfz 251/7 Ausf Ds. No other variant of the SdKfz 251 was ever equipped with these kinds of assault bridges. The crew compartment as well as the armor shield for the MG 42 machine gun were covered with canvas. The overall height of the SdKfz 251/7 engineer vehicle was 2.70 meters, which was .95 meters taller than the standard SdKfz 251/1 troop carrier.

The space between the two support brackets is filled with a wooden planking. A number of SdKfz 251/7s had this planking, but the main part of the engineer variant lacked of the wooden planking on the upper superstructure.

This assault bridge is on the right side. The bridges were capable of carrying any vehicle up to 8,000 kilograms, such as the SdKfz 251 half-track or a PzKpfw 38(t).

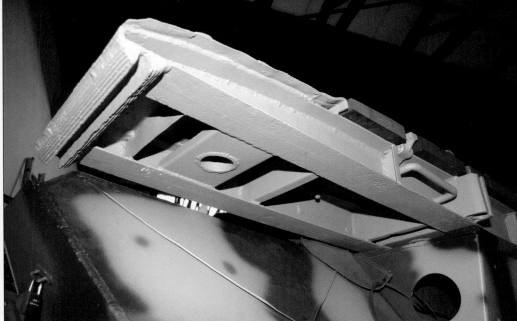

The rear lower surface of the right assault bridge has a welded-on handle so the crew can carry the bridge.

Each handle was welded on both sides in the front and rear section of the Übergangsschiene 8. These assault bridges had manufactured metal pieces. Four soldiers were needed to carry a single assault bridge.

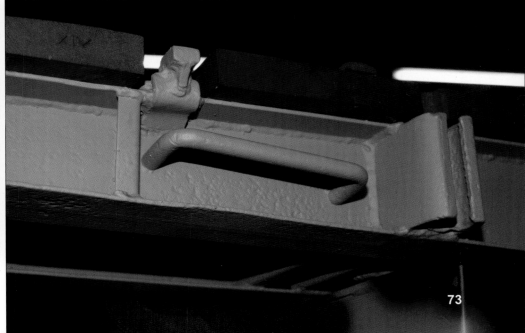

The rear arrangement of the right Übergangsschiene 8 rests on the support bracket. Note the circular aperture is located on the rear bracket.

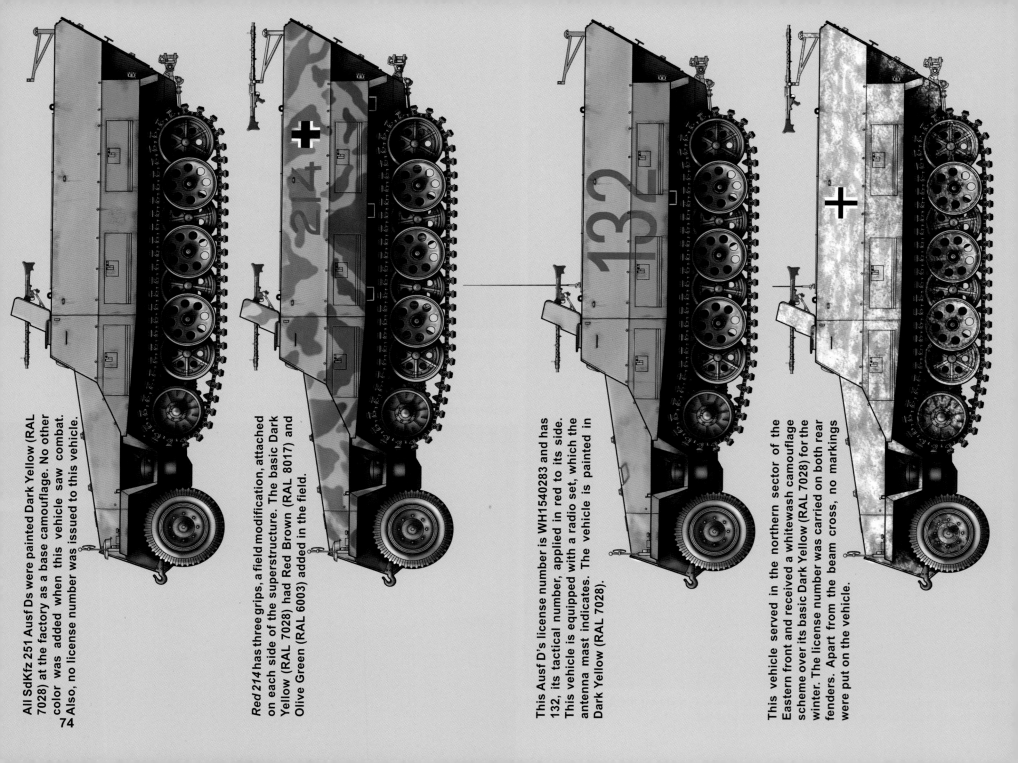

All SdKfz 251 Ausf Ds were painted Dark Yellow (RAL 7028) at the factory as a base camouflage. No other color was added when this vehicle saw combat. Also, no license number was issued to this vehicle.

74

Red 214 has three grips, a field modification, attached on each side of the superstructure. The basic Dark Yellow (RAL 7028) had Red Brown (RAL 8017) and Olive Green (RAL 6003) added in the field.

This Ausf D's license number is WH1540283 and has 132, its tactical number, applied in red to its side. This vehicle is equipped with a radio set, which the antenna mast indicates. The vehicle is painted in Dark Yellow (RAL 7028).

This vehicle served in the northern sector of the Eastern front and received a whitewash camouflage scheme over its basic Dark Yellow (RAL 7028) for the winter. The license number was carried on both rear fenders. Apart from the beam cross, no markings were put on the vehicle.

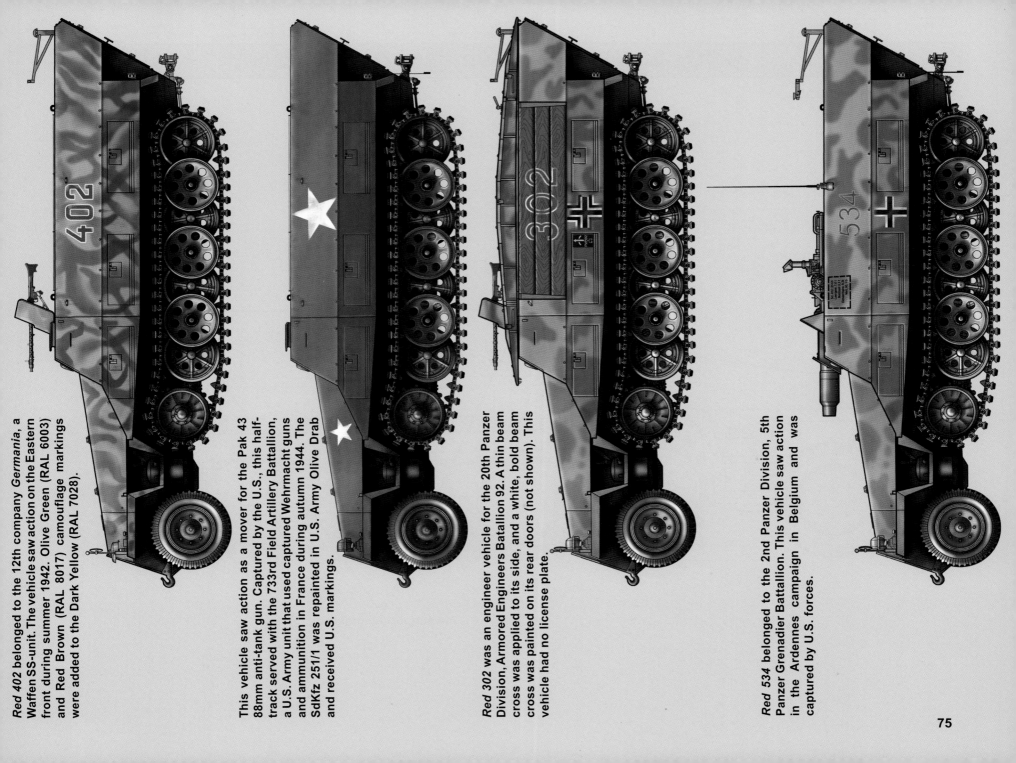

Red 402 belonged to the 12th company *Germania*, a Waffen SS-unit. The vehicle saw action on the Eastern front during summer 1942. Olive Green (RAL 6003) and Red Brown (RAL 8017) camouflage markings were added to the Dark Yellow (RAL 7028).

This vehicle saw action as a mover for the Pak 43 88mm anti-tank gun. Captured by the U.S., this half-track served with the 733rd Field Artillery Battalion, a U.S. Army unit that used captured Wehrmacht guns and ammunition in France during autumn 1944. The SdKfz 251/1 was repainted in U.S. Army Olive Drab and received U.S. markings.

Red 302 was an engineer vehicle for the 20th Panzer Division, Armored Engineers Batallion 92. A thin beam cross was applied to its side, and a white, bold beam cross was painted on its rear doors (not shown). This vehicle had no license plate.

Red 534 belonged to the 2nd Panzer Division, 5th Panzer Grenadier Batallion. This vehicle saw action in the Ardennes campaign in Belgium and was captured by U.S. forces.

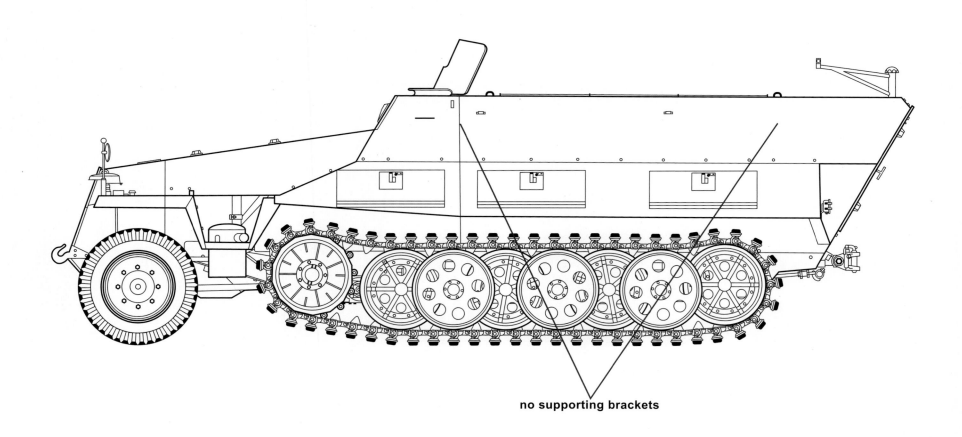

no supporting brackets

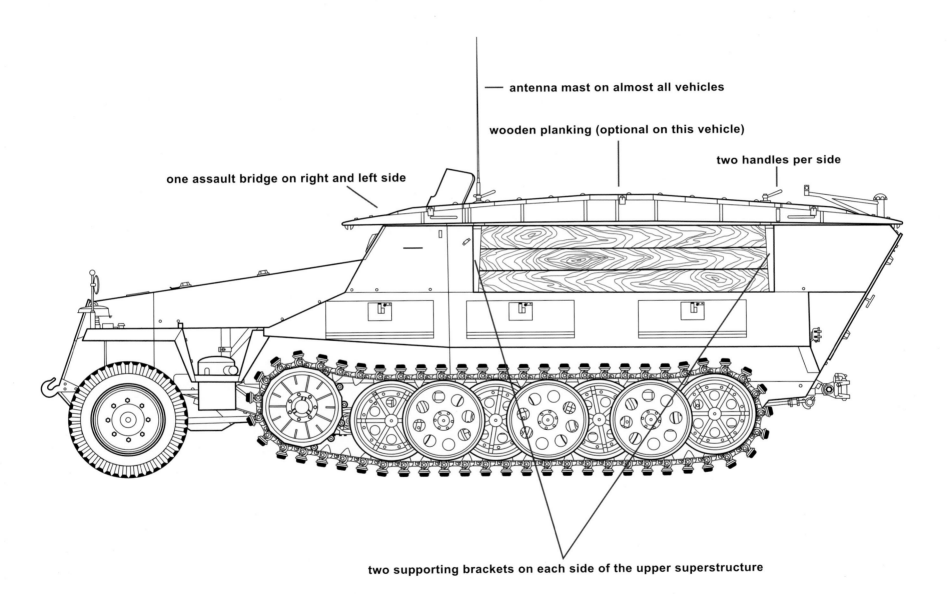

antenna mast on almost all vehicles

wooden planking (optional on this vehicle)

two handles per side

one assault bridge on right and left side

two supporting brackets on each side of the upper superstructure

The left superstructure on the engineer vehicle has wooden planking on the support brackets. The assault bridges have a curved shape. The metal pieces had a wood covering. Some Ausf Ds lacked assault bridges and carried other bulky equipment such as wooden laths, which were carried on the support brackets.

The wood upper surface of the Übergangsschiene 8 had transverse wooden pieces that were attached to the entire length of the assault rail's wood surface.

The rear right assault bridges shows that the leading part of the Übergangsschiene was metal while the remaining surface was wood-covered.

The assault bridges were secured to each of the four support brackets with a handle. The entire handle was connected with the support bracket and had to be removed from the decking before the assault bridge could be removed from the superstructure of the SdKfz 251/7 Ausf D.

Part of the engineer equipment carried in the crew compartment of the SdKfz 251/7 were mines. These mines were stored in special containers, as shown here. The SdKfz 251/7 Ausf D carried the same benches as the SdKfz 251/1 troop carrier.

The antenna socket was attached to the inner surface of the support bracket. Most SdKfz 251/7 Ausf D engineer vehicles were equipped with a radio, and thus carried an antenna socket with an antenna mast so the radios could be used.

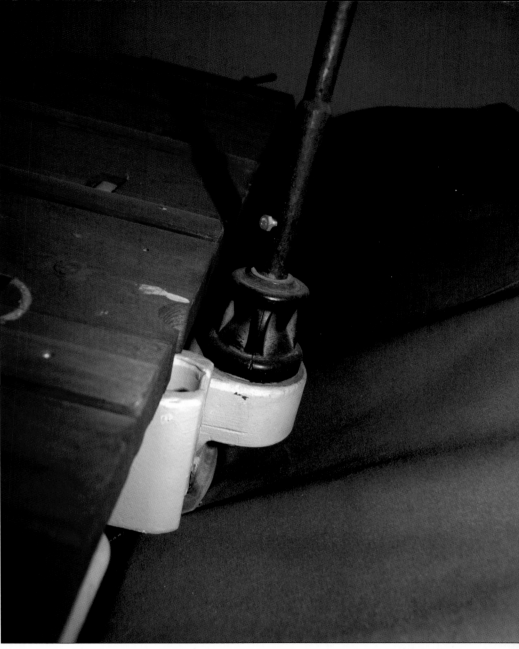

Most SdKfz 251/7 Ausf Ds carried a single antenna socket plus antenna mast attached on the right assault bridge at the front. The SdKfz 251/7 Ausf D on exhibit in the Panzermuseum at Munster had two antenna sockets. Apart from the standard location, the second antenna socket was located on the rear left assault bridge. This configuration of two antenna masts was very rarely seen in operation during WWII.

The SdKfz 251 Ausf Ds indeed allowed Panzergrenadiere to provide infantry support to Panzers. Despite the mass production of the Ausd D, however, the Wehrmacht never had enough of these vehicles to go around. In fact, several units had to settle for trucks as transportation.